Bodge Buster
Air Source Heat Pump Installation Advice

From our home to yours: Must-ask questions, real homeowner insights and a practical guide for a smoother heat pump experience.

Disclaimer
This book provides essential questions and insights that we, along with fellow homeowners, wish we had known when installing our heat pump. As a regular homeowner, without the qualifications of an installer or a professional in the heat pump industry, our aim is to share our firsthand real-world knowledge to smooth out your journey with a heat pump installation and help you sidestep the common pitfalls many encounter. However, it's crucial to understand that this book reflects our personal experiences and opinions only. Each property is unique, and the advice from your chosen installers should take precedence in your decision-making process. Treat this book as a friendly guide from one cosy home to another, rather than a set of definitive rules. We cannot be held responsible or liable for any outcomes or issues that might arise from your heat pump installation.

Renewable Heating Hub
Join the heat pump conversation at the Renewable Heating Hub website, a helpful and approachable community for homeowners interested in renewable heating. Share your experiences, ask questions and connect with others passionate about sustainable living. Visit the Renewable Heating Hub forums to become part of this growing community:
https://renewableheatinghub.co.uk/forums

© Mars Mlodzinski 2024

Contents

Introduction 5
Check Your Installer's Credentials 7
Right-Sized Heat Pump 9
Compare Quotes 11
Verify Installer Expertise 13
Radiators & Underfloor Heating 15
Overzealous Manufacturer Guarantees 17
Microbore Pipes 19
Groundworks & Planning 21
Grants & Incentives 23
Warranties & Guarantees 24
Ongoing Maintenance & Servicing 27
Noise Levels & Unit Placement 29
Project Timeline & Communication 31
Site Access & Disruption 33
Regulations & Standards 35
Professionalism 37
Safety & Compliance 39
Inspections & Certificates 41
Handover & System Training 43
Performance Monitoring & Optimisation 45
Remote Access 47
Troubleshooting & Support 49
Hot Water Cylinder 52
Weather Compensation 55
Coefficient of Performance (COP) 57
Defrost Cycles 59
Heat Pumps & Buffer Tanks 61
Lodging an Installation Complaint 63
Home Insurance 65
End of Life 67
Non-Negotiable Questions Your Installer Must Answer 69
Wrapping Up 71

Introduction

The air source heat pump (ASHP) promises not only greener heating but also the potential for lower heating bills. However, concerns about poor installations, subpar performance and high installation costs have made many UK homeowners hesitant.

In 2018, we moved into a rural Victorian farmhouse with an oil boiler and after extensive research and reading, we made the decision to install an ASHP. Back then, information about heat pumps, especially in layman's terms, was scarce, which meant we heavily relied on our installer's expertise for making key installation decisions. As a result, our installation was far from ideal; it was partially botched, leading to months of "teething issues" and two winters filled with challenges. Although our system functioned relatively well, it became evident over time that numerous aspects of the installation were subpar and could have been executed much more effectively. This experience highlighted the importance of attention to detail and the need for thoroughness in every aspect of the installation process, from initial system design planning to final execution.

All of these issues led us to create a website, Renewable Heating Hub, as an online platform for homeowner education, support and a place for us to share experiences.

This book is designed to empower you, the homeowner, to confidently navigate the world of ASHPs. We acknowledge the unsettling stories of bad installations and the confusion caused by technical jargon. This guide provides you with essential questions, insights and tips to help you get a better installation, optimise efficiency and unlock the true potential of this technology.

Our goal is not to turn you into a heat pump expert but to equip you with the knowledge to identify and avoid common missteps that lead to poor installations. More importantly, it equips you to actively engage with your installer, ensuring they adhere to the highest standards in installing both the heat pump and its supporting system.

It's essential to recognise that heat pumps *are* effective as a technology, and performance issues arise when they are poorly installed or incorrectly commissioned.

Since heat pump installations represent a significant financial investment, it's crucial for homeowners to take comprehensive precautions to secure a high-quality installation.

Check Your Installer's Credentials

Before signing any contracts or letting an installer anywhere near your home, it's crucial to verify their qualifications. Look for two key accreditations to begin with: Microgeneration Certification Scheme (MCS) for heat pumps and TrustMark endorsement.

Why MCS?
- Nationally recognised standard: MCS sets the standard for heat pump installations in the UK. Installers must meet technical requirements to achieve MCS accreditation, ensuring they possess the necessary knowledge and skills for a professional job.
- Peace of mind: Choosing an MCS-accredited installer provides you with assurance they understand the technology, follow best practices and comply with building regulations.
- Essential for government grants: If you're planning to use government grants for your heat pump installation, such as the Boiler Upgrade Scheme, or whatever scheme will follow in the future, choosing an MCS-accredited installer is mandatory.

Why TrustMark?
- Endorsement of quality: TrustMark is a government-endorsed quality scheme for home improvements. Their endorsement provides additional confidence that the installer operates with transparency, integrity and fair pricing.
- Consumer protection: TrustMark offers dispute resolution services, meaning you have recourse if any issues arise with the installation.

It's essential to recognise that MCS accreditation, while a significant marker of installer qualification, does not always guarantee a competent installer. MCS accreditation means that an installer has met certain industry standards and undergone a process to demonstrate their knowledge and compliance with the best practices in the installation of heat pumps (or other renewable technologies).

Despite these requirements, numerous homeowners on the Renewable Heating Hub forums have reported experiences with substandard installations carried out by MCS-accredited installers. These cases highlight that while MCS accreditation is an important consideration, it should not be the sole criterion in your decision-making process. It underscores the importance of conducting your own due diligence, such as checking online reviews, seeking references and having detailed discussions with potential installers about your specific needs and their approach to meeting them.

Action Steps
- Ask your potential installer for their MCS and TrustMark certificates. Verify their authenticity by checking the respective websites.
- Don't be afraid to compare quotes from multiple MCS-accredited and TrustMark-endorsed installers. Price shouldn't be the sole deciding factor.
- Ask in-depth questions about the installer's experience with heat pumps, their warranty offerings and after-sales support.

Search for installers through the MCS and TrustMark websites. These platforms allow you to filter by location, type of installation and certifications, making it easier to find qualified professionals in your area.

Right-Sized Heat Pump

Choosing the right air source heat pump for your home isn't a game of chance. Installing the wrong size or poorly designed system can lead to subpar performance, increased energy bills and even overheating or under-heating. That's why insisting on a detailed property survey and heat loss calculation before moving forward is crucial.

What is a Property Survey?

A qualified installer will visit your home and thoroughly assess its characteristics, including:
- Size and layout: Number of rooms, floor area and overall building footprint.
- Construction materials: Walls, roof, floors and windows - understanding their insulation levels is key.
- Existing system: Radiators, underfloor heating or any other existing elements influencing heat distribution.
- Hot water needs: Daily hot water usage will be factored into the system design.

What is a Heat Loss Calculation?

Based on the information gathered during the survey, the installer will perform a heat loss calculation using specialised software. This calculation determines how much heat your home loses through its various elements on a cold day. This is like taking your home's temperature and understanding how quickly it loses heat.

Why are These Aspects Important?

- Right-sized heat pump: An accurate heat loss calculation ensures you get the perfect size heat pump for your needs. Too small, and it won't adequately heat your home. Too large, and you'll waste energy and money. Don't let an installer propose a heat pump that's too large or too small.

- Optimal system design: The calculation informs the ideal layout and configuration of the heat pump system, including emitter size and placement, ensuring efficient heat distribution throughout your home.
- Maximised efficiency: Getting the right size and design leads to optimal performance and potentially lower energy bills. You'll be using just the right amount of energy to achieve the desired comfort level.

Action Steps
- Don't accept quotes or proposals without a survey and heat loss calculation. This is non-negotiable for a responsible heat pump installation.
- Ask the installer about their methodology for the survey and calculation. Understanding their approach helps ensure thoroughness and accuracy.
- Request a copy of the heat loss calculation report in writing. This document serves as valuable reference and helps hold the installer accountable for their recommendations.

Taking the time and insisting on a detailed survey and heat loss calculation is an investment in your long-term satisfaction and potential savings. It prevents costly mistakes and ensures you reap the optimal benefits of your air source heat pump.

Compare Quotes

Selecting the right air source heat pump installer requires careful consideration beyond just price. It's important to obtain at least three detailed quotes from different installers. These quotes should be comprehensive, clearly outlining all deliverables. Avoid settling for vague communications like a brief email or a price sent via text message. A well-documented quote ensures clarity and helps protect you from potential issues, ensuring you get the best value and quality for your investment.

Why Compare Quotes?

- Price transparency: Comparing quotes allows you to assess the market rate for similar installations in your area and avoid potential overpricing. Don't be afraid to request cost breakdowns.
- Quality assessment: Comparing proposed heat pump models and warranties gives you an insight into the installers' approach and commitment to quality.
- Finding the right fit: Each installer will have their own strengths, specialisations and heat pump brands they prefer working with. Comparing quotes helps you find the one that best aligns with your needs and budget.

What to Compare in Your Quotes

- Price: Consider the overall cost of the installation, including equipment, labour and any additional fees. Remember, the cheapest option isn't always the best - prioritise quality and value for money.
- Proposed heat pump models: Ask about the specific brand and models each installer recommends for your home. Research these models online and compare their efficiency, performance, noise and warranty terms.

- Warranties: Pay close attention to the length and coverage of the warranties offered by each installer. Look for comprehensive warranties that cover both parts and labour for a reasonable period.
- Additional services: Some installers may offer additional services like system maintenance or ongoing support. Compare these offerings and see if they align with your expectations. Some installers have fine print that states your warranty is void unless you purchase a service and maintenance package from their company.

Action Steps
- Contact at least three reputable installers in your area. Use online directories, recommendations or MCS's website to find qualified professionals.
- Be clear about your needs and budget during your initial communication. The more information you provide, the more accurate your quotes will be.
- Ask detailed questions about each quote. Don't hesitate to clarify any points of confusion or request further information. If something is unclear, keep asking the question until you fully understand the answer.
- Trust your gut: Consider factors beyond just price. Choose the installer that demonstrates thoroughness, professionalism and a clear understanding of your specific needs.

Taking the time to compare quotes is an investment in your long-term satisfaction. You'll be more confident in your decision, potentially secure a better deal and set yourself up for a successful heat pump experience.

Verify Installer Expertise

When entrusting your home's heating system to an air source heat pump installer, you want to be certain they have the knowledge and skills to deliver a flawless job. During your vetting process, verify that the installer has experience with the specific brand and model of the heat pump they are recommending. It's important to ascertain their proficiency in programming the ASHP for optimal use, rather than just relying on the factory default settings for heating and hot water.

Gather Details of Past Installations
- Request a portfolio: Ask the installer to provide you with a detailed list of similar heat pump installations they've completed in recent years. This should include information such as:
    - ✓ Project size and scope (type of property)
    - ✓ Brands and models of heat pumps installed
    - ✓ Challenges faced and solutions implemented
    - ✓ Customer feedback or testimonials
- Specific examples: Inquire about installations that closely resemble your own home's size, layout and heating needs. This will give you a better sense of their expertise in handling projects like yours.

Speak to Past Clients
- Request references: Ask for contact information of at least three past customers who have had heat pumps installed by the company.
- Engage in conversations: Reach out to these references and ask questions, such as:
    - ✓ Were they satisfied with the installation process and overall experience?
    - ✓ Did the installer meet deadlines and communicate effectively?

✓ Were they reliable and turned up when then they said they would?
✓ Did the installer stay on budget?
✓ Has the heat pump system performed as expected, providing comfort and efficiency?
✓ Did any issues arise, and if so, how did the installer handle them?
✓ Would they recommend the installer to others?

Verify Online Reputation
- Check reviews: Search for online reviews of the installer on independent platforms like Trustpilot, Google Business or local review sites.
- Look for patterns: Pay attention to the overall tone of the reviews, common themes and how the installer responds to any negative feedback.
- Consider ratings: While not always perfect, online ratings can provide a general sense of customer satisfaction.

Action Steps
- Prioritise experience: Don't be afraid to prioritise installers with a proven track record of successful heat pump installations.
- Value quality over quantity: A few stellar references can be more valuable than a long list of mediocre ones.
- Listen to your instincts: If you feel uneasy about an installer's experience, attitude or references, it's better to move on and explore other options.

A reputable installer will be happy to provide evidence of their expertise and connect you with satisfied customers. They should also be willing to answer all your questions. By taking the time to verify their experience, you increase your chances of a successful installation and long-term satisfaction with your heat pump system.

Radiators & Underfloor Heating

Installing an air source heat pump isn't a one-size-fits-all solution. Just like finding the perfect outfit, it's essential to ensure your chosen heat pump seamlessly integrates with your existing heating system and hot water needs. Incompatible systems can lead to headaches like uneven heating and underwhelming performance.

Radiator Compatibility
Not all heat pumps play nicely with existing radiators:
- Flow temperature: Traditional boilers operate at higher temperatures than most conventional low temperature heat pumps. Ensure your heat pump delivers the necessary flow temperature to comfortably warm your home through your existing radiators.
- Radiator size: Smaller radiators might not emit enough heat when paired with a heat pump. Consider upgrading to larger radiators if necessary. K3 radiators are strongly recommended for cold rooms that struggle to come to temperature.
- System balancing: Your installer should assess and potentially adjust your existing radiator system to ensure even heat distribution throughout your home. This should be a non-negotiable.

Underfloor Heating
If you have underfloor heating, it's usually a perfect partner for an air source heat pump. However, still ensure compatibility:
- Underfloor type: Certain types of underfloor heating, like electric mats, might be incompatible with heat pumps. Discuss alternatives with your installer if needed.
- Pipe spacing: The spacing of your underfloor heating pipes is crucial for effective heat transfer. Verify if your existing system aligns with the optimal spacing for your chosen heat pump.

Action Steps
- Be transparent: Clearly communicate your existing heating system type, radiator details (if applicable) and hot water needs to your installer.
- Seek expertise: Rely on your installer's knowledge and experience to recommend a heat pump compatible with your existing setup.
- Ask questions: Don't hesitate to inquire about flow temperatures, system adjustments and potential upgrades to ensure optimal performance.
- Ask the installer to justify installation decisions if something doesn't seem logical.

By investing time in ensuring system compatibility, you create a harmonious partnership between your air source heat pump and your existing heating and hot water systems, and avoid any nasty surprises when temperatures outside drop. This translates to comfort, efficiency and long-term satisfaction with your investment.

Overzealous Manufacturer Guarantees

While some heat pump installers and manufacturers might boast about their heat pumps offering comfort even at -25°C, remember it's the entire system, not just the heat pump, that determines your home's true comfort level in extreme temperatures. Focusing solely on the pump's capacity creates a potentially misleading picture, similar to the old boiler-centric approach in central heating systems.

The Crucial Role of the Sink System

Even the most powerful heat pump needs a well-designed "sink" system to efficiently distribute and retain heat throughout your house. Think of it as the final leg of the heat transfer journey. This system encompasses:
- Distribution network: Pipes, pumps and other components that carry the heated water throughout your home.
- Heat emitters: Underfloor heating, radiators or other elements that release the heat into the air.
- Control system: The brains of the operation, managing temperature, flow rates and energy efficiency.

The Pitfalls of Overlooking the Sink System

- Mismatched emitters: Undersized radiators or improperly configured underfloor heating can choke the system, preventing efficient heat distribution and leaving you shivering.
- Unbalanced flow rates: Too fast or too slow water flow can waste energy and compromise comfort.
- Inefficient control: An outdated or poorly programmed control system can lead to temperature fluctuations and energy spikes.

Prioritising a Holistic System Design

Instead of chasing unrealistic comfort guarantees based solely on pump specs, prioritise a holistic approach that considers all system components and your home's characteristics:

- Work with a competent installer: Choose someone who understands system design and can create a tailored solution for your home, considering your heat loss, existing infrastructure and ideal heating emitters like underfloor heating.
- Focus on system sizing and balance: Double check with the installer that the heat pump capacity, pipe dimensions and emitter sizes are optimally matched for efficient heat transfer and temperature control.
- Optimise flow rates: Push the installer to properly configure pumps and control settings to ensure the water flows at the right speed, maximising efficiency and minimising energy waste.

The heat pump is just one piece of the puzzle. By prioritising a well-designed distribution system and focusing on holistic system optimisation, you can unlock the true potential of your heat pump and achieve genuine comfort, even in challenging weather conditions. It's not just about pumping heat - it's about delivering it efficiently and strategically throughout your home.

Microbore Pipes

Living in a home from the 1980s or 1990s, you might come across an interesting aspect of your heating system: microbore pipes. These slender, cable-like pipes, often hidden in walls, have stirred up quite a bit of discussion about their compatibility with heat pumps. Let's clear some misconceptions and shed light on the reality of heat pump installations.

Beyond Size
Don't be swayed by installers who categorically claim "microbore pipes and heat pumps don't mix." In reality, the pipe's size isn't the ultimate decider; it's about design and precise calculations. In systems with microbore piping, installers must strategically manage flow rates, which often involves integrating additional pumps into the system. This can result in a marginally higher cost for pumping.

Optimising Heat Distribution
Picture your house as a network of water highways. Large rooms with high-demand radiators need wider pathways (thicker pipes) for adequate heat distribution. Smaller rooms are fine with narrower pipes. Heat pumps, known for their efficiency, push water through these pipes briskly, providing 'quick' heating at lower temperatures.

Here's a simple comparison:
- Modern Boilers: They're like cruising on Easy Street. Their slow flow and high temperatures work well with most existing pipework.
- Heat Pumps: They amp up the water flow, which might necessitate some system tweaks. A skilled and competent installer will survey your home's pipe network, room by room, using precise calculations to ensure compatibility with the heat pump's flow requirements.

It's important to remember that pipe sizing in the past wasn't always as exact as it is today. Some areas in your home might have microbore pipes that are actually larger than necessary, while others might need a bit of an upgrade. A knowledgeable installer, using accurate calculations, can determine whether your system needs any modifications, like installing more robust pumps or additional pipes, to ensure your home stays comfortably warm.

Microbore piping isn't a roadblock to efficient heat pump installation. Seek a comprehensive assessment from your installer. They're equipped to navigate through your home's pipe layout, crafting a solution that delivers efficient and comfortable heating, even with those narrower pipes.

Groundworks & Planning

Before your air source heat pump journey begins, it's crucial to understand if any groundworks or planning permission is necessary. Neglecting these details can lead to unexpected delays, additional costs and even potential legal complications.

Groundworks
- Trenching: In most installations, the outdoor unit and indoor system need to be connected with electrical cables and piping. If the unit is located farther from the main house, this connection will likely involve trenching through your garden or property.
- Foundations: Depending on the chosen unit and ground conditions, a concrete base or mounting brackets might be needed for the outdoor unit.
- Drainage Solutions: Proper drainage prevents flooding and ground ice around the outdoor unit and ensures efficient operation. Discuss any necessary drainage channels or gravel beds with your installer.

Planning Permission
- Generally Permitted: In most UK cases, installing an ASHP falls under permitted development rights, meaning planning permission isn't typically required.
- However, there are exceptions:
    - ✓ Listed buildings or their curtilage
    - ✓ Conservation areas
    - ✓ Flats or shared buildings
    - ✓ Installations impacting external appearance

- Always Check: Verify local regulations and consult your council's planning department. It's better to be safe than sorry. Planning permission requirements can vary slightly depending on your location.

Cost Considerations
- Groundworks: The installer should outline the specific groundworks needed and associated costs in the quote. Negotiate a clear breakdown of charges for trenching, foundations, materials, heat loss pipes and drainage solutions.
- Planning Permission Fees: If planning permission is needed, you'll incur application fees. Factor these into your budget estimations.

Action Steps
- Discuss Groundworks: Ask your installer for a detailed plan of any required groundworks and a clear cost breakdown. Ensure they factor in potential challenges like underground obstacles or complex garden layouts.
- Check Planning Requirements: Don't assume an automatic exemption. Contact your local council's planning department to confirm if planning permission is needed for your specific installation.
- Be Informed: Knowing the potential groundworks and planning needs empowers you to budget accurately, avoid surprises and ensure a smooth installation process.

By delving into the details of groundworks and planning permission, you lay the groundwork for a stress-free and compliant installation. It's essential to address these aspects upfront to avoid potential headaches and unexpected costs down the line.

Grants & Incentives

Installing an air source heat pump is an investment, but several government grants and financial incentives can significantly reduce your upfront costs.

Boiler Upgrade Scheme
- At time of writing in 2024, this scheme offers grants of up to £7,500 for installing a ground source or air source heat pump for homeowners in the UK.
- You must own the property and replace an existing fossil fuel system to qualify.

Explore Further Options
- Some energy suppliers offer cash back deals or discounts for ASHP installations. Contact your supplier for details.
- Check with your local council for potential grant schemes or support programmes for renewable energy investments.
- Keep an eye out for other government schemes that incentivise homeowners to move away from fossil fuel heating systems.

Action Steps
- Visit the Boiler Upgrade Scheme website (or whichever scheme replaces it in the future) to check your eligibility and apply.
- Contact your energy supplier to inquire about ASHP offers.
- Check your local council's website or contact them directly about renewable energy incentives.
- Stay informed about potential RHI developments to benefit from future financial support.

Warranties & Guarantees

Investing in a heat pump is a long-term commitment, and ensuring your investment is protected is very important. That's where warranties and guarantees come in, but navigating the fine print can sometimes be tricky.

Manufacturer Warranties
- Coverage: Manufacturer warranties typically cover parts and labour for a specific period. Some might also include coverage for specific components like the compressor or inverter.
- Terms and conditions: Read the warranty document carefully to understand any exclusions, limitations or requirements to maintain coverage. This might include regular servicing or specific installation conditions.
- Registration: Some warranties require registering your heat pump with the manufacturer within a specific timeframe to activate coverage. Don't forget to do this.

Installer Guarantees
- Workmanship: A reputable installer will offer a guarantee on their workmanship, typically lasting 1 to 2 years. This covers any faults or issues arising from the installation itself, such as faulty connections or leaks.
- Parts: Some installers might also offer an additional guarantee on specific parts they install, separate from the manufacturer's warranty.
- Dispute resolution: Understand the process for resolving any issues covered by the installer's guarantee. Ask about their customer service procedures and dispute resolution channels.

Action Steps
- Compare warranty terms: When comparing air source heat pump models, ask for detailed warranty information from each manufacturer. Consider the length of coverage, exclusions and registration requirements.
- Clarify installer guarantees: Before signing any contracts, ensure you understand the terms of the installer's guarantee for workmanship and any additional parts coverage. Get it in writing.

Understanding warranties and guarantees empowers you to make informed decisions and choose the best protection for your heat pump investment. Don't hesitate to ask questions, read the fine print and choose an installer with a solid reputation for quality workmanship and reliable after-sales support.

Make Your Own Notes Here:

Ongoing Maintenance & Servicing

Your air source heat pump is a system with many moving parts, and like any high-performance machine, it requires regular upkeep to ensure optimal performance, efficiency and longevity.

Maintenance Schedules
Annual Servicing: Most manufacturers recommend annual servicing by a qualified engineer. This service typically involves:
- ✓ Checking refrigerant levels and pressure.
- ✓ Cleaning filters and condenser coils.
- ✓ Assessing system performance and efficiency.
- ✓ Identifying potential issues or wear and tear.
- ✓ Keep the area around the outdoor unit clear of debris and ensure its fan(s) isn't obstructed.

Cost Considerations
- Annual Service: Costs can vary depending on the region, installer and specific model. Expect to pay around £150-£250 for a basic annual service, but we have seen instances where homeowners have been charged in excess of £400.
- Repairs: While not commonplace with proper maintenance, unexpected repairs can occur. Costs will depend on the nature of the problem and replacement parts needed.

Action Steps
- Schedule your first service: Contact your installer to schedule your first annual service after installation so it's booked and in your diary.
- Ask about maintenance requirements: Discuss the recommended maintenance schedule for your specific model with your installer or manufacturer.

- Budget for ongoing costs: Factor the annual service cost into your household budget, and consider setting aside a contingency fund for potential repairs.
- Monitor performance: Stay alert for any changes in your air source heat pump's performance, such as noise levels, energy consumption or reduced heating output. Early detection of potential issues can save you money on repairs.

Regular maintenance isn't just about keeping your heat pump running smoothly; it's an investment in its long-term performance, efficiency and reliability. By understanding your maintenance needs and proactively addressing them, you can enjoy the benefits of your heat pump for years to come.

Noise Levels & Unit Placement

Living with an air source heat pump should be comfortable and peaceful, offering consistent temperature control, energy efficiency and low noise levels, thus creating a serene and sustainable home environment.

Understanding Noise Levels
- Decibels (dB): Sound is measured in decibels, with higher numbers being louder. A whisper is around 30 dB, while a normal conversation is about 60 dB.
- ASHP Noise: Modern units are quite quiet, typically around 40-60 dB at 1 metre, similar to a dishwasher or microwave.
- Distance Matters: Noise decreases with distance. Consider the distance between the outdoor unit and your windows or bedrooms for minimal disturbance.

Finding the Ideal Location
- Regulations: Check your local regulations for air source heat pump placement, minimum distances from property lines and noise restrictions. This ensures your unit doesn't disturb neighbours or violate any building codes.
- Aesthetics: Choose a location that blends in with your outdoor space:
    - ✓ Visibility: Can shrubs or fencing partially screen the unit?
    - ✓ Access: Easy access is crucial for servicing and maintenance.
    - ✓ Wind direction: Consider prevailing wind patterns to minimise noise impact.

Sidewall Installations
If you're considering installing your air source heat pump against the side of your house, it's important to invest in high-quality vibration

mounts. These specialised mounts effectively absorb and isolate vibrations generated by the unit, preventing them from transmitting and reverberating through the house walls and causing noise or discomfort inside.

Action Steps
- Ask your installer about noise levels: Get the specific noise level of your chosen model and inquire about noise reduction options if needed.
- Review local regulations: Familiarise yourself with any rules regarding air source heat pump placement and noise limits in your area.
- Plan your placement carefully: Consider all the factors mentioned above and discuss different options with your installer.
- Talk to your neighbours: If the unit is close to a property line, inform your neighbours beforehand and address any concerns they might have.

Balancing regulations, aesthetics and low noise impact is key to a successful air source heat pump installation. By carefully considering these points and communicating effectively, you can enjoy a quiet and cosy home with your new eco-friendly heating system.

Project Timeline & Communication

Installing an air source heat pump is a multi-step process, and clear communication and a well-defined timeline are crucial for a smooth and successful journey.

Key Steps in the ASHP Installation Process
- Initial Survey and Assessment: Your installer will conduct a thorough survey of your property to assess suitability, measure dimensions and determine specific requirements.
- System Design and Planning: They'll design the system layout, select appropriate components and obtain any necessary permits or approvals.
- Equipment Delivery: The air source heat pump unit and associated equipment will be delivered to your property, ready for installation.
- Internal Installation: This involves connecting the unit to your existing heating system, including pipework, wiring and controls.
- External Unit Installation: The outdoor unit will be carefully positioned, levelled and connected to the indoor components.
- Electrical Connections: A qualified electrician will connect the heat pump to your electrical supply and install any necessary safety features.
- Commissioning and Testing: The installer will commission the system, ensuring it operates correctly and efficiently.
- Handover and Training: You'll receive a comprehensive handover, covering system operation, maintenance and troubleshooting.

Setting Expectations and Timeline
- Discuss expected timeframes upfront: Ask your installer for a detailed timeline outlining each stage's duration, including potential

delays due to weather, equipment availability or unforeseen issues. Also ask how long you may be without central heating and hot water - there *will* be a downtime.
- Factor in lead times: Consider any potential lead times for equipment delivery, especially during peak seasons.
- Review the schedule: Ensure you understand and agree on the proposed timeline, and raise any concerns or scheduling conflicts early on.
- Confirm in writing: Get the agreed-upon timeline in writing, including expected start and completion dates, as part of your contract.

Communication Protocols
- Designate a point of contact: Establish a primary contact person for both you and the installation team to ensure clear communication channels.
- Agree on preferred communication methods: Discuss preferred methods (phone, email, text, etc.) and frequency of updates.
- Proactive updates: Encourage your installer to provide regular updates on progress, any delays or changes to the schedule.
- Raise concerns promptly: If you have any questions or concerns throughout the process, don't hesitate to communicate them clearly and promptly.

A well-defined timeline and open communication create a foundation for a successful heat pump installation. By setting clear expectations, staying informed and addressing any concerns promptly, you can navigate the process with confidence and look forward to enjoying the comfort and efficiency of your new heating system on schedule.

Site Access & Disruption

Bringing an ASHP into your home involves preparation and ensuring smooth access for installation.

Securing Site Access

- Clear a Path: Ensure clear access for the installer's team and equipment to the installation site, both indoors and outdoors. This includes doorways, hallways and the area around the chosen location for the outdoor unit.
- Parking and Delivery: Discuss parking arrangements for the installation team and delivery vehicles for equipment. If necessary, obtain temporary permits for street parking if space is limited.
- Utilities Access: Identify and mark the location of underground utilities (gas, water, electricity, etc.) near the installation site to avoid accidental damage during digging or trenching.

Minimising Disruption

- Water Supply Access: Confirm the location of your main water shutoff valve to enable temporary water shutoff during internal plumbing connection for the air source heat pump. This minimises potential disruption to your water supply.
- Power Outages: Discuss the possibility of temporary power outages during electrical connection for the unit. Ask your installer about the duration and timing of such outages to minimise inconvenience.
- Dust and Noise Control: Be prepared for some dust and noise during installation, especially with outdoor work. The installer should use dust sheets and minimise unnecessary noise to ensure a more comfortable experience.
- Cleanup and Restoration: Ensure your installer includes post-installation cleanup and restoration in their contract. This should

involve removing construction debris, re-positioning furniture and ensuring the work area is left clean and tidy.

Action Steps
- Talk to your installer: Discuss your property layout, access points and any potential challenges early on.
- Clear the installation area: Remove furniture or obstacles that might impede access to the chosen locations.
- Communicate with neighbours: If necessary, inform your neighbours about potential parking limitations or brief disruptions during the installation process.
- Be present for key stages: Consider being present on-site during crucial steps like water shutoff or electrical connection to address any immediate concerns.

By clearly communicating your needs, ensuring proper access and planning for potential disruptions, you can pave the way for a smooth and efficient heat pump installation with minimal inconvenience. Don't hesitate to discuss any concerns or preferences with your installer upfront to ensure a seamless transition to your new eco-friendly heating system.

Regulations & Standards

As mentioned numerous times, adding an air source heat pump to your home is an investment in sustainable comfort. But just like any construction project, ensuring the quality of materials is crucial for long-term performance, safety and peace of mind.

Building Regulations
- UK Building Regulations: All installations must comply with relevant UK building regulations for heating systems, electrical works and safety standards. These regulations ensure the system is installed safely, efficiently and meets performance requirements.
- Building Control Notifications: Depending on the scope of your installation, you might need to notify your local building control authority beforehand. Your installer should guide you through this process.

Material Quality Standards
- Industry standards: Ask your installer about the materials they use and whether they meet recognised industry standards for pipework, insulation and electrical components.
- Manufacturer guarantees: Check if the materials used come with guarantees from reputable manufacturers, offering additional assurance of quality and durability.
- Independent certifications: Look for any third-party certifications for the materials or the installer's practices, such as CE marking for components or environmental certifications for sustainable sourcing.

Action Steps
- Discuss building regulations: Ask your installer to explain how they will ensure your ASHP installation complies with all relevant UK building regulations.
- Ask about material standards: Inquire about the specific standards and certifications for the materials they use.
- Request written documentation: Keep written records of any certifications and guarantees.

By choosing an installer who prioritises quality materials and sustainable practices, you can contribute to a greener future while enjoying the long-term benefits of your eco-friendly heating system.

Professionalism

Bringing an air source heat pump into your home involves trusting experts to manage the installation process.

Professionalism
- Punctuality and Communication: Expect the installation team to arrive on time, communicate proactively about progress and any unforeseen issues, and be courteous and respectful throughout the project.
- Qualified and Certified: Ensure the team members are qualified and certified for their respective tasks, including electrical work, plumbing and heat pump installation.
- Safety First: Observe safe working practices by the team, including the use of appropriate personal protective equipment and adherence to safety regulations.
- Problem-solving & Adaptability: Anticipate the team's ability to address unforeseen challenges during the installation and adapt to unforeseen circumstances while maintaining professional conduct.

Cleanliness and Tidiness
- Protected Workspaces: Expect the team to lay down protective sheets and covers in both indoor and outdoor work areas to minimise dust and debris spread.
- Waste Management: Observe proper disposal of construction waste, including packaging materials, old equipment (if replaced) and any debris generated during the installation process.
- Final Cleanup: Ensure the team leaves the work areas clean and tidy upon completion, removing all protective coverings, tools and leftover materials.

- Respect for Property: Expect the team to treat your property with respect, minimising damage or wear and tear during installation and promptly addressing any accidental issues.

Action Steps
- Set expectations upfront: Discuss your expectations for professionalism and cleanliness with your installer before the project begins.
- Communicate openly: Don't hesitate to voice any concerns about hygiene, mess or unprofessional behaviour to the team or your installer.
- Monitor progress: Keep an eye on the work area, noting how waste is managed and whether safety protocols are followed.
- Provide feedback: After the installation is complete, share your feedback with your installer about your experience, both positive and negative, to help them improve their service.

By setting clear expectations, communicating openly, and providing feedback, you can ensure your chosen installer prioritises professionalism, respects your property and leaves you with a clean and comfortable haven to enjoy your new, eco-friendly heating system.

Safety & Compliance

Peace of mind is essential when welcoming an air source heat pump into your home.

Key Regulations and Codes
- UK Building Regulations: These regulations govern various aspects of construction, including heating systems, electrical work, insulation and safety standards. They ensure your heat pump installation is safe, efficient and meets performance requirements.
- Part L of Building Regulations: Specifically addresses energy efficiency in buildings, ensuring your heat pump contributes to reducing carbon emissions and complies with energy-saving measures.
- Electrical Safety Standards: The installation of electrical components must conform to the Wiring Regulations, safeguarding against electrical hazards and ensuring safe operation.
- Gas Safety (if applicable): If your air source heat pump is part of a hybrid system involving gas appliances, the installer must comply with Gas Safety (Installation and Use) Regulations (GSIUR) to prevent gas leaks and ensure safe operation.
- Product-Specific Standards: The air source heat pump unit and associated components must meet relevant product standards, such as British Standards (BS) or European CE marking, guaranteeing their quality and safety.

Your Installer's Responsibilities
- Knowledge of Regulations: Your installer should have a thorough understanding of all applicable regulations and codes.
- Compliance Planning: They should plan the installation to meet all requirements and obtain any necessary permits or approvals from local building control authorities.

- Documentation: They should provide you with documentation demonstrating compliance, such as certificates of installation or building control notifications.

Your Role as a Homeowner
- Ask for Confirmation: Before starting the installation, ask your installer to confirm their commitment to complying with all relevant regulations and codes.
- Request Documentation: Ask for copies of certificates or documentation demonstrating compliance.
- Building Control Notifications: If required, your installer should guide you through notifying your local building control authority about the installation.
- Independent Inspections: You have the right to seek independent inspections from qualified professionals to verify compliance if you have any concerns.

Compliance with regulations isn't just about passing inspections; it's about ensuring your heat pump's system is safe, efficient and meets performance standards. By choosing a reputable installer who prioritises compliance and taking an active role in the process, you can safeguard your home and protect your investment.

Inspections & Certificates

With your air source heat pump installation nearing completion, ensuring all final inspections and certifications are in place is crucial for smooth operation and peace of mind.

Understanding Required Inspections and Certifications
- Building Control Notification: Depending on the scope of your installation, your local building control authority might require notification and subsequent inspection to confirm compliance with relevant building regulations. Your installer should guide you through this process.
- Electrical Certificates: All electrical work associated with the heat pump installation must be inspected and certified by a qualified electrician, typically issuing an Electrical Installation Certificate (EIC).
- Product Warranties and Guarantees: To activate manufacturer warranties and installer guarantees, specific completion certificates or documentation might be required. Ensure you understand any necessary actions from your installer or manufacturer.

Who Arranges the Inspections and Certifications?
- Building Control: Your local building control authority usually handles their own inspection process, and you might need to pay a fee for it. Your installer should guide you on the timeline and any required actions.
- Electrical Certificates: Your chosen electrician is responsible for arranging and issuing the EIC for the electrical work.
- Product Warranties and Guarantees: Consult your installer or manufacturer regarding any specific documentation or completion certificates required to activate warranties and guarantees.

Action Steps for Homeowners
• Confirm required inspections: Before the installation begins, clarify with your installer which inspections are required and who will arrange them.
• Ask about certificates: Inquire about any completion certificates or documentation needed for warranties, guarantees or incentive claims.
• Keep records: Secure copies of all inspection certificates, completion documents and warranties for future reference.
• Be informed: Don't hesitate to ask your installer or local building control authority any questions you have about the required inspections and certifications.

By taking an active role, understanding your responsibilities and working with your trusted installer, you can ensure your new heating system receives its official "green light" and operates safely and efficiently for years to come.

Handover & System Training

Congratulations! Your air source heat pump installation is complete, and you're on the cusp of experiencing a cosy, eco-friendly home. But before diving into comfort, ensure you receive a comprehensive handover and system training to operate your new unit confidently and efficiently.

What to Expect During Handover

- System Demonstration: Your installer should walk you through the installed system, highlighting key components like the outdoor unit and control panel. They should explain how each component works in concert to provide heating and hot water.
- Operational Instructions: Receive a clear and concise explanation of how to operate your heat pump's controls. Learn how to adjust temperature settings, access weather compensation, set schedules, switch between heating and hot water modes, and access advanced features like vacation mode or boost functions.
- Maintenance Guidance: Understand routine maintenance tasks like cleaning filters and identifying potential warning signs. Ask the installer about the recommended frequency for each task and any specific protocols for your system.
- Emergency Protocols: Be informed about what to do in case of unexpected occurrences like system glitches, power outages or equipment malfunctions. Your installer should explain how to identify and troubleshoot common issues and provide contact information for support in case of more serious problems. Ask if there is a manual to help you decode any system error codes.
- This is also a good time to ensure that your weather compensation is activated on your heat pump.

Beyond the Basics: Deepening Your Knowledge

- Request user manuals: Ask your installer for copies of the user manuals for your specific heat pump model and any additional components installed. These manuals provide detailed instructions, troubleshooting tips and technical specifications for further reference.
- Explore online resources: Many air source heat pump manufacturers offer online resources like tutorial videos and FAQs. Immerse yourself in these resources to gain an even deeper understanding of your system and discover helpful tips and tricks.
- Stay connected with your installer: Don't hesitate to reach out to your installer if you have any questions or concerns after the handover. Establishing a good relationship with your installer ensures you have a reliable source of expertise and support throughout your heat pump journey.

Benefits of a Smooth Handover and Training

- Confident and efficient operation: Knowing how to control your ASHP effectively translates to optimal comfort and energy efficiency. You'll feel empowered to adjust settings and utilise features for maximum benefit.
- Peace of mind: Understanding maintenance procedures and emergency protocols alleviates worry and prepares you to handle minor issues on your own.
- Reduced dependence on technicians: By mastering basic troubleshooting, you can potentially avoid unnecessary technician visits and save on costs.

By actively participating in this process, asking questions, and seeking additional resources, you can become a confident owner and operator, unlocking the full comfort and efficiency of your eco-friendly heating system.

Performance Monitoring & Optimisation

Once your air source heat pump is humming away, keeping your home cosy, your journey to optimal performance is just starting. Embracing performance monitoring and optimisation opens the door to maximising efficiency, minimising energy consumption and squeezing the most out of your investment.

Monitoring Options

- Built-in system controls: Many heat pumps come equipped with basic monitoring features through their control panels. These can display key data points like room temperature, hot water temperature, outdoor temperature and system operating mode.
- Dedicated heat pump monitoring systems: Consider independent monitoring systems that offer comprehensive data collection and analysis. These systems often provide insights into advanced metrics like coefficient of performance (COP), flow rates and even system health indicators.

Optimisation Techniques

- Fine-tuning settings: Based on your performance data, you can adjust temperature set points, operating schedules and advanced parameters like flow rates and defrost settings to optimise efficiency for your specific needs and usage patterns.
- Weather compensation: Most ASHPs offer weather compensation features that adjust heating output based on outdoor temperature, reducing unnecessary energy consumption on milder days. Ensure that the installer has activated this.
- Hot water management: Optimising hot water schedules and temperatures, prioritising heating over hot water during peak

demand periods, and considering alternative hot water solutions like solar thermal can significantly impact overall system efficiency.
- System maintenance: Regular maintenance tasks like cleaning filters and ensuring proper air flow around the outdoor unit contribute to optimal performance and prevent energy losses.

Benefits of Monitoring and Optimisation
- Reduced energy consumption: By identifying and eliminating inefficiencies, you can potentially achieve significant energy savings, lowering your bills.
- Enhanced comfort: Fine-tuning your system based on your data ensures consistent and optimal temperature levels, maximising your comfort throughout the year.
- Extended system lifespan: Proactive identification of potential issues through data analysis allows for early intervention and preventative maintenance, extending the life of your ASHP.
- Informed decision-making: Data-driven insights empower you to make informed choices about future system upgrades or adjustments, ensuring your ASHP continues to meet your needs efficiently.

Taking Action
- Discuss monitoring options with your installer: Explore built-in features, consider upgrading to smart controls (provided that they don't adversely interfere with system), and investigate dedicated monitoring systems based on your budget and desired level of detail.
- Ask your installer about potential optimisation techniques: They can analyse your data, suggest adjustments to settings, and recommend best practices for maximising efficiency based on your specific system and usage patterns.
- Become an active data watcher: Don't shy away from exploring your monitoring system and understanding the data it provides. The more you engage with your system's performance, the more opportunities you discover for optimising its efficiency and comfort.

Remote Access

Imagine adjusting your home's temperature, monitoring energy consumption or switching heating modes all from the comfort of your smartphone, no matter where in the world you are.

Remote Access Options

• Built-in Wi-Fi: Many modern heat pumps boast built-in Wi-Fi capability, allowing you to connect directly to your system through a dedicated app on your smartphone or tablet. These apps typically offer basic control features like temperature adjustments, schedule settings and operational mode switching.

• Smart thermostats and controllers: Upgrading to a smart thermostat or controller unlocks a wider range of functionalities. Connect with popular ecosystems like Google Home, Apple HomeKit or Amazon Alexa for voice-activated controls. Access advanced features like geofencing to automatically adjust settings based on your location, or integrate with other smart home devices for personalised comfort scenarios.

• Third-party monitoring systems: Dedicated heat pump monitoring systems offer the most comprehensive remote access experience. These systems not only allow for control but also provide detailed performance data, historical trends and real-time energy consumption insights, empowering you to make data-driven optimisation decisions.

Compatibility Considerations

• Air source heat pump model and manufacturer: Not all ASHPs are equipped with built-in Wi-Fi, and compatibility with specific smart thermostats or monitoring systems can vary. Ensure your chosen technology aligns with your heat pump model and brand capabilities if you'd like remote access.

- Your home network and infrastructure: A reliable Wi-Fi connection is crucial for seamless remote access. Consider your internet bandwidth and potential coverage limitations in different parts of your home when choosing a remote control solution.
- Personal preferences and desired features: Prioritise functions that align with your lifestyle and comfort needs. Do you crave basic remote control, or do you desire detailed performance data and advanced automation options? Choose a solution that offers the features you value most.

Benefits of Remote Access and Control

- Convenience and comfort: Adjust your home's temperature, preheat before arriving, or switch modes remotely - all at your fingertips. Enjoy optimal comfort even when you're not there.
- Enhanced efficiency: Remote access allows for data-driven optimisation. Analyse energy consumption, adjust schedules based on occupancy patterns and identify potential inefficiencies for maximum savings.
- Peace of mind: Monitor your system's performance remotely, receive alerts for potential issues and schedule preventative maintenance for a worry-free experience.
- Sustainable living: Optimising your system's efficiency through remote access and control not only saves energy but also reduces your carbon footprint, contributing to a greener future.

Action Steps

- Consult your installer: Discuss your remote access preferences and explore compatible options based on your specific ASHP model and home network infrastructure.
- Research various solutions: Compare features, functionalities, and compatibility of different apps, smart thermostats, and monitoring systems to find the perfect fit for your needs and budget.
- Embrace the possibilities: Don't hesitate to experiment with remote control features and explore automation options. The more you engage with your system, the more opportunities you discover for maximising comfort, efficiency, and convenience.

Troubleshooting & Support

Even the most reliable air source heat pump might encounter occasional hiccups. The key to minimising disruption and ensuring swift resolution lies in understanding the troubleshooting process and establishing clear communication channels with your installer and support network.

Support Network
- Initial warranty period: Most air source heat pump installations come with a comprehensive warranty covering parts and labour for a defined period. During this time, your installer is the main point of contact for any troubleshooting needs.
- Extended warranties: Consider investing in an extended warranty or maintenance plan for continued peace of mind beyond the initial warranty period. These plans often offer priority service and reduced costs for repairs or maintenance.
- Manufacturer support: Some manufacturers offer additional support channels, such as dedicated helplines or online troubleshooting resources. This can be a valuable resource, especially if your installer is unavailable or the issue lies with a specific system component.
- There are also free resources to get support like the forums at Renewable Heating Hub.

Troubleshooting Process
- Initial assessment: If you encounter an issue with your heat pump, first try simple troubleshooting steps like checking system settings, ensuring adequate power supply and restarting the unit. Refer to your user manual for specific instructions and troubleshooting tips if there's an error code on the control panel.

- Contacting your installer: If basic troubleshooting doesn't resolve the issue, contact your installer. Clearly explain the problem you're experiencing and any error messages or indicators you've observed.
- Diagnostic and evaluation: Your installer will likely conduct a diagnostic evaluation to identify the source of the problem. This may involve reviewing performance data, inspecting system components and potentially running diagnostic tests.
- Repair or resolution: Depending on the diagnosis, your installer will recommend appropriate repair solutions or propose alternative remedies.

Clarifying Response Times
- During warranty period: Discuss typical response times for troubleshooting and repair during the initial warranty period with your installer upfront. This ensures you have realistic expectations in case of an issue.
- Out-of-warranty scenarios: Response times and service fees for repairs outside the warranty period may vary depending on the nature of the problem and your installer's scheduling availability. Clarify these details in advance to avoid surprises.
- Emergency situations: Most installers offer emergency support for critical issues that pose a risk to property or safety. Understand the process for contacting them in such situations and ensure they are aware of your emergency contact information.

Proactive Measures
- Regular maintenance: Regularly scheduled maintenance by your installer can help prevent potential problems and identify minor issues before they escalate.
- Familiarise yourself with your system: Spend time understanding your heat pump's control panel, basic operational principles and common error codes. This empowers you to handle minor issues yourself and communicate more effectively with your installer.
- It's crucial to know the location of the main filter in your system, as many errors and faults in heat pump systems often stem from a blocked filter. Regular monitoring and maintenance of this filter are essential for smooth operation.

- Maintain open communication: Don't hesitate to contact your installer with any questions or concerns you might have about your ASHP, even if it's just for clarification. Building a strong relationship with your support network ensures you receive timely and effective assistance when needed.

A minor hiccup with your heat pump doesn't have to disrupt your comfort. By understanding the troubleshooting process, establishing clear communication with your installer and taking proactive measures, you can navigate any potential issues calmly and efficiently, ensuring your heating system delivers reliable comfort for years to come.

Hot Water Cylinder

Your air source heat pump isn't just about keeping spaces warm and cosy; it's also responsible for providing your home with a steady flow of hot water. But for this dynamic duo to tango in perfect harmony, compatibility between your heat pump and hot water cylinder is crucial.

Assessing Your Existing Cylinder
- Capacity and performance: Consider the size and performance capabilities of your existing cylinder. Does its capacity match your hot water demand, especially with the additional load of the air source heat pump? If you have a large household or frequently experience hot water shortages, upgrading to a larger cylinder might be necessary.
- Material and insulation: The type of material your cylinder is made of (copper, stainless steel, etc.) and its insulation level can impact its efficiency. Older cylinders might lose heat faster, requiring your heat pump to work harder and potentially impacting its efficiency.
- Coil compatibility: The cylinder's internal coil, which transfers heat from the heat pump to the water, must be compatible with your model and operating temperatures. Consult your installer on this. In most cases, if you have an old water cylinder, this will be upgraded to a compatible option.

Considering Upgrade Options
- Dedicated ASHP cylinders: Some manufacturers offer hot water cylinders specifically designed for optimal performance with their ASHPs. These cylinders often feature larger coils, improved insulation and pre-configured settings for seamless integration.

- Solar thermal integration: Consider harnessing the power of the sun by integrating a solar thermal system with your ASHP and hot water cylinder. This can significantly reduce your reliance on electricity for hot water generation, leading to substantial energy savings.
- Solar PV: If you have an existing solar PV array, you want to consider getting a diverter that uses excess solar production to heat your hot water.

Matching for Optimal Performance
- Prioritise efficiency: Choose a cylinder with good insulation and a coil size optimised for your ASHP's output. This minimises energy consumption and maximises hot water availability. If in doubt, speak to your installer about this.
- When using an air source heat pump, it's advisable to avoid heating your domestic hot water above 45C to maintain system efficiency. Additionally, make sure to discuss with your installer the frequency of the Legionnaires' disease prevention cycle.
- Future-proof your system: Consider your potential hot water needs in the coming years. If your family is growing opt for a cylinder with some extra capacity for future expansion.
- Seek expert advice: Consulting your installer is crucial for evaluating your existing cylinder's compatibility and recommending the best upgrade options for your specific needs and heat pump model.

Your hot water cylinder plays a vital role in your heat pump's overall performance. Don't underestimate the importance of compatibility. By assessing your existing cylinder, exploring upgrade options, and seeking expert advice, you can ensure your heat pump and hot water supply dance in perfect harmony, delivering comfort, efficiency and peace of mind for years to come.

Make Your Own Notes Here:

Weather Compensation

Your air source heat pump, enhanced with weather compensation technology, purrs away quietly, seamlessly adjusting to the ever-changing outdoor temperatures. It efficiently draws warmth from the air, ensuring your home remains comfortable, dynamically adapting to keep you snug and warm, no matter how the weather fluctuates outside.

Understanding Weather Compensation

Imagine your traditional heating system like a dial set to one temperature, regardless of the weather outside. This is like baking a cake at the same heat for both a delicate soufflé and a dense loaf of bread - that's inefficient and inconsistent.

Weather compensation acts like a smart thermostat, constantly monitoring the outdoor temperature and adjusting your ASHP's heat output accordingly. On milder days, it reduces energy consumption by supplying less heat. On colder nights, it ramps up the warmth for optimal comfort.

Why Weather Compensation Matters

This dynamic duo of air source heat pump and weather compensation delivers tangible benefits:
- Reduced energy bills: By generating only the required heat, weather compensation can decrease your electricity costs by up to 30% compared to fixed settings.
- Extended ASHP lifespan: Avoiding unnecessary high-temperature operation minimises wear and tear, potentially saving you on costly replacements down the line.
- Consistent comfort: With heat output adapted to the outside temperature, weather compensation ensures stable room temperatures, eliminating unpleasant chills or stuffy afternoons.

Don't Settle for Fixed Set Points

Some installers, prioritising ease over efficiency, might opt for setting your heat pump to a constant flow temperature, such as 45C, to preclude complaints about cold radiators, irrespective of the actual outdoor temperature. This one-size-fits-all approach, while convenient for the installer, overlooks the nuanced efficiency that weather compensation can provide. Weather compensation, often underutilised, is your silent efficiency expert, dynamically adjusting the heat output based on external temperatures. By enabling and properly configuring this feature for your specific system and home environment, you ensure that your heat pump operates optimally, providing comfort without unnecessary energy expenditure.

Cooler Radiators: Don't Panic!

With weather compensation, your radiators might feel cooler or lukewarm compared to fixed set points over 40C. This doesn't mean your home is colder. Think of it this way: a well-insulated house loses heat slowly, so lower radiator temperatures can still effectively maintain your desired comfort level. Trust weather compensation and if rooms are still too cool for your liking, you can ask your installer to assist you in adjusting your heat curves.

Embrace the Power of Weather Compensation

Weather compensation is more than just a technical feature; it's a key ingredient in unlocking your heat pump's full potential. By understanding its benefits, insisting on its activation and trusting the cooler radiators as a sign of efficiency, you can enjoy consistent comfort, minimise energy bills and reduce your carbon footprint, all while living sustainably.

Before your installer completes the job, ensure that they balance the system and calculate a heat curve specifically tailored to your house. This curve should determine the lowest flow temperature necessary to maintain your home at a comfortable 21C. This step is crucial for optimising the efficiency and effectiveness of your heating system.

Coefficient of Performance (COP)

Your air source heat pump might seem like a magic box that conjures warmth from cold air. But behind this magic lies a crucial number: the Coefficient of Performance (COP).

What is COP?
COP is a metric that gauges the efficiency of your heat pump. It indicates how much heat is produced for each unit of electricity consumed. For instance, a COP of 3 means that for every single unit of electricity used, your air source heat pump generates three units of heat. This ratio is crucial for understanding and maximising the efficiency of your heat pump.

Why Does COP Matter?
A higher COP indicates a more efficient system. Essentially, this means:
- Lower energy bills: A higher COP translates to less electricity needed to generate the same amount of heat, potentially leading to significant cost savings in the long run.
- Reduced carbon footprint: Lower energy consumption also means a smaller environmental impact, making your ASHP a more sustainable choice.
- Optimal performance: Understanding the COP under different weather conditions helps you choose a model that performs efficiently throughout the year, even in colder climates.

Unmasking the COP Mystery
- Model-specific COP: Always inquire about the specific COP of the ASHP model you're considering. Manufacturers typically provide COP ratings at different outdoor temperatures to give you a comprehensive understanding of its efficiency across seasons.

- COP in real-world conditions: Remember that advertised COPs might not always reflect real-world performance. Factors like house size, insulation level and system installation can affect the actual COP achieved. Consult your installer for an estimated COP based on your specific home and climate.
- Seasonal COP: Look for the seasonal COP, which considers the average COP throughout the year for your climate zone. This gives you a more accurate picture of your ASHP's overall efficiency.

Become a COP Champion

Understanding the COP empowers you to make informed decisions about your ASHP and choose the model that delivers the perfect balance of comfort, efficiency and sustainability. By prioritising COP during your selection process and consulting with your installer, you can ensure your ASHP not only warms your home but also warms your heart with the satisfaction of knowing you've made a wise choice for both your wallet and the planet.

Remember, the COP is your key to unlocking the true efficiency potential of your air source heat pump. Don't settle for an efficiency mystery - be an informed homeowner, ask about the COP, and choose the model that champions sustainable comfort for years to come.

Defrost Cycles

Air source heat pumps enter defrost cycles to maintain efficiency and functionality in cold weather. During winter, frost can accumulate on the outdoor unit. This buildup reduces the heat pump's ability to absorb heat from the outside air, impacting its efficiency.

The defrost cycle temporarily reverses the heat pump operation, warming the outdoor coils to melt the frost and restore normal operation. This process is essential for the ASHP's longevity and ensures it continues to heat your home effectively, even in colder conditions.

Methods
- Reverse-cycle defrost: This common method temporarily reverses the refrigerant flow, turning the indoor unit into the evaporator and melting the frost with its generated heat. The melted water then drains away, and the outdoor unit resumes normal operation.
- Hot gas defrost: This method uses hot refrigerant gas directly from the compressor to melt the frost, offering faster defrosting times but potentially consuming more energy.

Defrosting's Impact
While crucial for maintaining efficiency, defrosting cycles do consume additional energy. This impact is particularly pronounced in colder weather when frost accumulates more quickly. The type of defrosting method and the frequency of cycles are key factors influencing energy consumption.

Minimising the Chill on Your Bills
- Choose wisely: Opt for an ASHP model with optimised defrosting algorithms that minimise defrosting frequency and duration.

- Weather compensation: Activate weather compensation on your ASHP to adjust heat output based on outdoor temperature, potentially reducing frost build-up and the need for defrosting.
- Regular Maintenance: Schedule routine inspections and maintenance of your heat pump to ensure optimal performance, which can help in early detection of issues that might lead to increased defrosting needs.

Heat Pumps & Buffer Tanks

In the ever-evolving landscape of home heating, technologies are constantly being challenged, improved and sometimes rendered obsolete. One such element facing scrutiny is the use of buffer tanks in conjunction with air source heat pump systems. As a homeowner, it's important to understand why the previously recommended practice of using buffer tanks is now seen by some as outdated and inefficient for most modern heating systems.

Outdated Narrative

Historically, buffer tanks were pivotal in the heating industry. They were introduced as a solution for the limitations of on-off fossil fuel boilers. These boilers operated at high temperatures (above 80C) to prevent corrosion in the heat exchanger. The high temperature operation was efficient for the technology at the time, and blending down through a buffer tank was advantageous. Additionally, these older systems required a low flow rate, contrasting with the higher demand from numerous circuits connected to them. The separation provided by buffer tanks allowed for more effective handling of these differing requirements. However, this is a story rooted in the past, not the present.

Misconception About Heat Pumps and Buffers

The idea that buffer tanks help heat pumps "smooth out load" is a growing misconception. In reality, a buffer tank's contribution to managing the load is minimal. For instance, a 100-litre buffer can hold merely 1.17kW of energy at a temperature 10C higher than required. If the system's load is 10kW, this translates to about 7 minutes of buffer time, which is not significant. Moreover, achieving that extra 10C in temperature can increase energy bills by up to 25%.

Modern Heating Landscape

Today's heating systems, equipped with modulating boilers and heat pumps, are designed for efficiency and precise control. In such systems, any form of buffering or system separation actually diminishes performance due to blending down. The argument for buffers in these advanced systems is outdated.

Manufacturer Recommendations

It's also notable that some manufacturers still recommend buffers and system separation. This practice often stems from a design limitation in the heat pumps themselves. Many units come with a small pump, incapable of adequately supplying heat to the entire system at the correct flow rate. Instead of addressing this issue at its core, manufacturers recommend the installation of a buffer tank. This approach is more a workaround than a solution, and it can often mask underlying design inadequacies.

Moving Beyond Buffers

When considering the installation of a heat pump as a homeowner, it's important to be aware that while buffer tanks have traditionally been a staple in heating systems, technological advancements have diminished their necessity. However, many installers in the UK still commonly recommend them. This trend can make the process of finding an installer who is willing to set up a heat pump system without a buffer tank somewhat challenging.

It's crucial to engage in thorough discussions with your installer to ensure that you make an informed decision. This conversation should focus on what best serves the efficiency and cost-effectiveness of your home's heating system. While some scenarios may still benefit from the inclusion of a buffer tank, in many modern setups, especially with advanced heat pumps, they may no longer be essential.

For those who are interested in understanding more about this topic, especially regarding the role of buffer tanks in heat pump systems, I recommend visiting the Renewable Heating Hub website where we have published detailed articles, complete with supporting data, to highlight the potential inefficiencies that can arise in systems equipped with buffer tanks.

Lodging an Installation Complaint

If you encounter a poorly executed heat pump installation, remember that as a homeowner, you have certain rights and options for recourse, but it's important to approach this with a realistic mindset. Theoretically, the processes for resolution appear straightforward, but in practice, they often fall short.

Our experience in assisting numerous homeowners with substandard installations has revealed the inefficiencies within the complaint's system. Entities like MCS and consumer codes, designed to safeguard homeowners, frequently pass responsibilities among themselves without providing effective solutions. This bureaucratic shuffle not only tests homeowners' patience but also drains their energy, often leading to a point of resignation. It's a disheartening reality in the industry that needs to be acknowledged and addressed.

Therefore, it's absolutely essential to take every precaution to ensure your heating system is installed correctly and avoid the struggle of dealing with a poorly executed installation.

Here's a streamlined guide to lodging a complaint:

Gather Evidence

- Contract and documentation: Collect all paperwork related to the installation, including quotes, invoices, contracts, deliverables, warranties and emails.
- Photo and video record: Document any visible issues with the installation, such as poor workmanship, leaks or damage.
- Performance monitoring: Track temperature readings, energy consumption and any significant performance discrepancies from promised efficiency.

Contact the Installer
- Initial communication: Attempt to resolve the issue directly with the installer. Clearly communicate the problems you've encountered and request rectification.
- Follow-up in writing: Keep a record of communications by sending emails or letters outlining the issues and proposed solutions.

Seek Third-Party Support
- MCS: If the installer is MCS-certified, their work is backed by a warranty scheme. Contact the MCS and lodge a complaint to initiate an investigation.
- Trading Standards: Trading Standards investigate unfair trading practices. If you suspect misrepresentation or poor workmanship, consider contacting them.
- Contact the consumer codes:
    - ✓ RECC: If your installer is RECC-certified, their independent dispute resolution service provides additional protection.
    - ✓ HIES: HIES members also offer a dedicated complaints procedure.
- Independent engineers: Hiring an independent engineer to assess the installation can provide professional validation of your concerns.

Legal Action
- Small Claims Court: For disputes under £30,000, consider using the Small Claims Court. Legal costs are lower, and you can represent yourself.
- Solicitors: In more complex cases, consult a solicitor specialising in construction or consumer law. They can advise on available legal options and represent you in court.

Home Insurance

Before proceeding with the installation, it's essential to update your home insurance policy. While most policies cover basic heating systems, it's important to verify whether yours includes coverage for air source heat pumps, as many policies still have exclusions for these types of systems. In the event that your current policy does not cover air source heat pumps, it's advisable to consider amending your coverage. Adding this specific protection ensures that your investment is safeguarded against unforeseen events such as damage or theft.

Here's the Scoop
- Existing coverage might not be enough: Standard home insurance policies may not automatically cover heat pumps.
- Additional coverage might be needed: Some insurers offer optional add-ons for heat pumps, providing extra peace of mind. Consider fire, theft and breakdown protection, because heat pumps and replacement parts can be very expensive.
- Don't leave it to chance: Contact your insurer directly or check their online portal to see if your current policy covers heat pumps and what additional options might be available.

Why it Matters
- Unexpected costs can bite: Imagine a malfunction or damage occurring to your heat pump or its compressor. Without proper coverage, you could be left facing substantial repair bills.
- Peace of mind is priceless: Being aware that your heat pump is protected allows you to enjoy its warmth without concerns over potential financial burdens. Surprisingly, despite their bulk and size, there have even been reports of air source heat pumps being stolen, so the more protection you have, the better.

Take Action
- Pick up the phone: Give your insurer a call and ask about their heat pump coverage options.
- Go online: Many insurers offer online policy management tools where you can easily check and update your coverage.
- Shop around: If your current insurer doesn't offer suitable heat pump coverage, consider comparing quotes from other providers.

A little proactive planning can save you a lot of hassle and expense down the line. So, before you fire up your heat pump, make sure your insurance is ready to keep you warm and worry-free!

End of Life

Like all good things, even your air source heat pump will eventually reach the end of its journey.

Disposal

Traditionally, disposing of an ASHP meant sending it to landfills, risking the release of harmful materials and contributing to environmental pollution. Thankfully, responsible disposal and recycling options are increasingly available, minimising waste and preserving valuable resources.

Decommissioning

Before your ASHP takes its final bow, a proper decommissioning process is crucial:
- Contact a qualified technician: Ensure a certified professional disconnects the system safely and removes any remaining refrigerant, preventing environmental hazards.
- Documentation is key: Collect documentation on the system's components and disposal options to ensure proper handling and compliance with local regulations.

Recycling

The good news is that many heat pump components are recyclable:
- Metals: The majority of the system's metal components, like copper and aluminium, can be processed and reused in new products, reducing the need for virgin materials.
- Plastics: Certain plastic components can be recycled into new plastic products, depending on local facilities and specific materials.
- Refrigerant: Improper refrigerant disposal poses environmental risks. Licensed technicians can recover and reclaim leftover refrigerant for repurposing in other systems.

Green Goodbye
- Research available options: Contact your local municipality, waste management companies, installers or ASHP manufacturers to identify recycling facilities or programmes in your area.
- Choose responsible partners: Ensure any chosen services are licensed and adhere to environmentally responsible practices for handling and processing materials.
- Compare the costs: While responsible disposal might involve added costs compared to traditional methods, consider the long-term environmental benefits and potential resource recovery value.

Legacy of Eco-Consciousness

By understanding and choosing responsible end-of-life practices for your ASHP, you can ensure its final act is as eco-friendly as its years of service. Recycling valuable materials, preventing pollution and minimising landfill waste allows you to contribute to a more sustainable future, leaving a legacy of environmental responsibility even after your ASHP retires from active service.

Non-Negotiable Questions Your Installer Must Answer

Having delved into the various aspects of air source heat pump installations in this book, it's clear that certain questions are pivotal to ensuring a successful and efficient setup.

These are the questions you absolutely must not forget to ask your installer. They are designed to cover all key areas of concern, from installation specifics to post-installation support, ensuring you are fully informed and prepared as you embark on this important journey.

Remember, asking the right questions is not just about getting answers; it's about gaining confidence and clarity in the process of installing your air source heat pump.

- Contract and Documentation Inquiry: Ask your installer about the specifics of the contract, including details about quotes, invoices and warranties. This ensures that you have a complete understanding of what is being agreed upon.
- Heat Pump Sizing and Heat Loss Calculations: Ask the installer how they determined the appropriate size for the heat pump in relation to your home's specific heat loss calculations? Make them walk you through the process to ensure the system is neither under nor oversized for your needs? This question ensures that the installer carefully considers the unique thermal characteristics of your home, leading to a more efficient and effective heating system.
- Buffer Tank Necessity: Discuss the necessity and implications of a buffer tank with your installer. Understand how it affects the system's efficiency and whether it's a requisite for your specific setup.
- Performance Monitoring: How will the system's performance be monitored and verified against the promised efficiency? Ensure that

the installer provides methods for tracking temperature readings and energy consumption, or how they can be accessed via the heat pump's control panel.
• Rectification and Follow-up: What are the procedures for rectifying any issues that arise post-installation, and how will these communications be documented?
• Installer Certification and Warranty: If your installer is MCS-certified, inquire about the warranty scheme and how it protects your installation.
• Independent Dispute Resolution Services: Ask if your installer is RECC-certified or a member of HIES, and understand how these affiliations provide additional protection in case of disputes.
• Handover Process: Ensure that the installer walks you through the system during handover, explaining key components such as the outdoor unit and control panel.
• Operational Instructions: Ask for clear and concise instructions on operating the heat pump's controls, including adjusting temperature settings, setting schedules, and accessing advanced features like vacation mode or boost functions. Also ask if there's a manual that covers common error codes.
• Weather Compensation Activation: Confirm that the weather compensation feature is activated on your air source heat pump. This feature is crucial for optimising energy efficiency and comfort. Double and triple check that this has been done.
• Maintenance Guidance: Inquire about routine maintenance tasks, such as cleaning filters, and the recommended frequency for each task. Ensure you understand any specific protocols for your system.
• Design Liability and Professional Indemnity Coverage: Inquire about the installer's responsibility for the full design of the system and whether they have professional indemnity insurance. This is essential to cover any potential issues arising from design flaws or installation errors. Ask for details about the scope of their coverage and how it protects you as a homeowner.

Wrapping Up

Throughout this book, we have navigated the intricacies of selecting, installing and optimising air source heat pumps, equipping you with the knowledge to make informed decisions about your home heating system. Remember, the path to sustainable and efficient home heating is not just about embracing new technology; it's about empowerment. By asking the right questions, insisting on quality installations, and understanding the nuances of your system, you are not just installing a heating unit; you are investing in the future of your home and the environment.

Your journey with your heat pump doesn't end with the last page of this book. It evolves as technology advances and as your understanding deepens, and I want to extend my sincere thanks for investing your time in reading this book. I hope that the information provided has been enlightening and will serve you well in your endeavours. Remember, every small step towards sustainability is a step towards a better future for us all.

In closing, I warmly invite you to become a part of our vibrant community at the Renewable Heating Hub forums: https://renewableheatinghub.co.uk/forums. This forum is a gathering place for homeowners like you, where you can share your experiences, seek answers to your pressing questions, or simply narrate the story of your own heating system journey. It's an opportunity to connect with others, to learn and to contribute to a community that is passionate about renewable heating solutions. Join us in shaping a greener, more sustainable future together.

Make Your Own Notes Here:

Make Your Own Notes Here:

Printed in Great Britain
by Amazon